Romania

Learning fun for young kids

By Author Jamie Pedrazzoli

All rights reserved, Copyright 2019 by Jamie Pedrazzoli AKA Author Jamie Bach

This ebook is licensed for your personal enjoyment only. This ebook may not be re-sold or given away to other people. If you would like to share this book with another person, please purchase an additional copy for each recipient. If you're reading this book and did not purchase it, or it was not purchased for your use only, then please return to Smashwords.com or your favorite retailer and purchase your own copy. Thank you for respecting the hard work of this author.

ISBN: 9781794432710

This book is dedicated to my beautiful daughters.

Buna, or Hello.

My name is Lavinia Marinescu.

Have you heard of Romania? It is located in Europe.

I live in the capital city of Bucharest.

Here is what my town looks like.

I like to ride the train. Have you ever been inside a train?

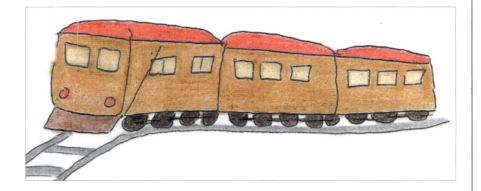

My favorite place to visit is the Bigar Waterfall.

This waterfall is magical to me. It seems like a fairy tale brought to life.

There are many castles in Romania.

There are also a lot of museums. This is the Gold Museum. Have you ever been to a museum?

The Carpathian Mountains are found in Romania.

There are even muddy volcanos here!

Would you ever want to see one of these?

My brother is going to tell you more about Romania.

Buna, or hello, my name is Alexandru Melosovici.

I want to tell you about some of the animals in Romania.

There are wolves.

There are bears.

There are also chamois. They may remind you of a goat. They are my favorite animals. What is your favorite animal?

These children are wearing some traditional outfits.

Have you heard of Dracula? His castle can be found in the Transylvanian Mountains! He was not really a vampire though, he was just a King that some people feared, and his name was Vlad III.

Dacian King Decebel is carved into a rock on the bank of the Danube River and is the tallest rock sculpture in Europe.

There are many famous Romanian people. Perhaps you have heard of Nadia Comaneci? She was the first gymnast to score a perfect 10!

Do you play any sports?

Here is our flag. My favorite color is yellow. What is your favorite color?

This is a photo of the tunnel of love. It is an abandoned train track.

Well, it is time for me to go eat breakfast now. Thank you for listening to us speak about our country, Romania.

**

Here are some Romanian Phrases.

How are you? Ce mai faci (chay-my-fatch)

School –şcoală (schkwa-la)

Games- jocuri (joe-koo-ree)

Friends-prieteni (Pree-uh-ten)

Food- alimente (ah-lee-men-tay)

Goodbye – La revedere (lah-rev-ay-day-ray)

The End.

Other books available include:

Around the World Series:

Denmark

India

Costa Rica

Romania

Zambia

Vietnam

And Germany

For kids and young adults:

Tongue twisting alphabet fun with Koby Jack and Bogart

Counting shapes and color fun with Koby Jack and Bogart

My jungle adventure in Costa Rica

Jess the Fox (also in Spanish) Jess el Zorro

Florida girls

Florida girls 2

Let's learn site words Kindergarten

Books For Adults or Teens:

Aleida Orphan no more a Cinderella story with a twist

Words of encouragement and how to cope with what life brings you

Untrusting Eyes

School for the Enchanted

About the Author

Jamie Pedrazzoli (Jamie Bach) grew up in Vero Beach Florida where she spent time taking art classes in high school with the

Center for the Arts Museum. She always enjoyed reading and writing.

She has two daughters that help inspire her to write.

"I'm so glad to be able to share my books with the world, I hope everyone enjoys reading them" she says.

**

Check out her websites and other links to social media.

Amazon sites

https://www.amazon.com/Jamie-Pedrazzoli/e/B07CN8F748

http://www.amazon.com/Jamie-Bach/e/B00LP37ZK4

Author site on facebook

https://www.facebook.com/jamiebachauthorchildrensbooks

Author site

http://authorjamiebach.weebly.com

Twitter

https://twitter.com/jamiebach421

Adventure Blog

http://theadventuresofkobyjackandbogart.weebly.com

Remember if you wish to contact this author an email address is provided. Do not call her or her parents' home. This is an invasion of privacy and is not appreciated. If it is of urgent importance EMAIL is the best way.

That email again is pedrazzolij@yahoo.com

The author is a very busy person so please understand that you may not get a response right away. Have patience. Thank you.

Made in the USA
Lexington, KY
25 June 2019